T. H. James

The Cub's Triumph

T. H. James

The Cub's Triumph

ISBN/EAN: 9783744704168

Printed in Europe, USA, Canada, Australia, Japan

Cover: Foto ©Thomas Meinert / pixelio.de

More available books at **www.hansebooks.com**

JAPANESE FAIRY TALE SERIES. No. 12.

THE CUB'S TRIUMPH.

Told in English by Mrs. T. H. James.

日本昔噺第十二號

野干ノ手柄

英國デヰムス夫人編述

定價金十五錢

明治十九年十二月七日 版權免許
同 二十年 一月 出版

東京府平民
出版人 長谷川武次郎

東京京橋區南鍋町二番地

凸版所 弘文社

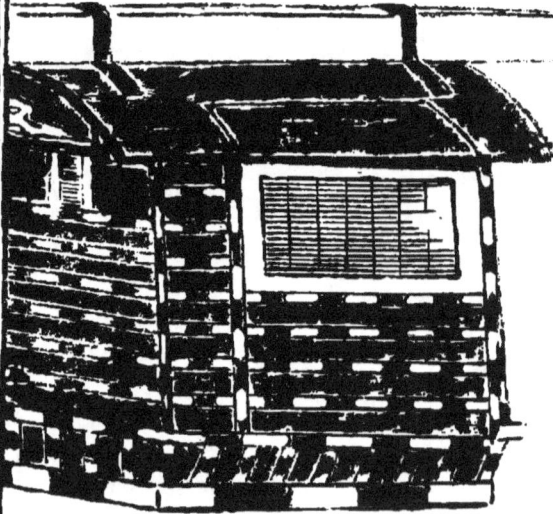

THE
CUB'S TRIUMPH.

ONCE upon a time there lived in a forest, a badger, and a mother fox with one little cub. There were no other beasts in the wood, because the hunters had killed them all with bows and arrows, or by setting snares.

The deer, and the wild boar, the hares, the weasles and the stoats, even the bright little squirrels had been shot, or had fallen into traps. At last, only the badger, and the fox, with her young one were left. And they were starving, for they dared not venture from their holes for fear of the traps.

They did not know what to do, or where to turn for food. At last the badger said,

"I have thought of a plan.

I will pretend to be dead. You
must change yourself into a man.
and take me into
the town, and
sell me.

With the money you get for me you must buy food, and bring it into the forest. When I get a chance, I will run away, and come back to you, and we will eat our dinner together. Mind you wait for me, and don't eat any of it until I come. Next week it will be your turn to be dead, and my turn to sell, do you see?"

The fox thought this plan would do very well: so, as soon as the badger had lain down, and pretended to be dead, she said to her little cub,

"Be sure not to come out of the hole until I come back. Be very good and quiet, and I will soon bring you some nice dinner."

She then changed her-self into a wood-cutter,

took the badger by the heels, and swung him over her shoulders, and trudged off into the town. There she sold the badger for a fair

price, and with the money bought some fish, some *tofu** and some vegetables. She then ran back to the forest as fast as she could, changed herself into a fox again, and crept into her hole to see if little cub was all right. Little cub was there, safe enough, but

very hungry, and wanted to begin
upon the *tofu* at once.

"No, no," said the mother fox.

"Fair play's a jewel. We must
wait for the badger."

Soon the
badger
arrived,
quite
out
of breath with running

so fast.

"I hope
you haven't
been eating any of
the dinner," he panted. "I could
not get away sooner. The man you
sold me to, brought his wife to
look at me, and boasted how

cheap he had bought me. You should have asked twice as much. At last they left me alone, and then I jumped up, and ran away as fast as I could."

The badger, the fox and the cub now sat down to dinner, and had a fine feast, the badger taking care to get the best bits for himself.

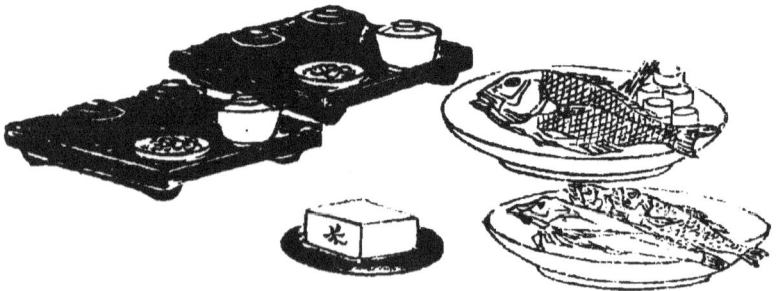

Some days after, when all the food was finished, and they had begun to get hungry again, the badger said to the fox;

"Now it's your turn to die." So the fox pretended to be dead, and the badger changed himself into a hunter, shouldered the fox, and went off to the town, where he made a good bargain, and sold her for a nice little sum of money.

You have seen already that the badger was greedy and selfish. What do you think he did now?

He wished to have all the money, and all the food it would buy for himself, so, he whispered to the man who had bought the fox.

"That fox is only pretending to be dead; take care he dosn't run away."

"We'll soon settle that", said the man: and he knocked the fox on the head with a big stick, and killed her.

The badger next laid out the money in buying all the nice things he could think of. He carried

them off to the forest, and there
eat them all up himself, without
giving one bit to the poor little
cub, who was all
alone, crying

for its mother, very sad, and very hungry.

Poor little motherless cub! But being a clever little fox, he soon began to put two and two together, and at last felt quite sure that the badger had, in some way, caused the loss of his mother.

He made up his mind that he would punish the badger; and, as he was not big enough, or strong enough, to do it by force, he was obliged to try another plan.

He did not let the badger see

how angry he was with him, but said in a friendly way.

"Let us have a game of changing ourselves into men. If you can change yourself so cleverly that I cannot find you out, you will have won the game; but, if I change myself so that you cannot find me out, then I shall have won the game. I will begin, if you like; and, you may be sure, I shall turn myself into somebody very grand while I am about it."

The badger agreed. So then,

instead of changing himself at all,
the cunning little cub just went
and hid himself behind a tree,
and watched to see what would
happen. Presently, there came

along the bridge, leading into the town, a *daimio*, seated in a *nori-mono*, a great crowd of servants and men at arms following him.

The badger was quite sure that
this must be the fox;
so, he ran up to the *norimono*,
put in his head, and cried.

"I've found you out!

I've won the game!"

"A badger! A badger! Off with his head," cried the *daimio*.

So one of the retainers
cut off the badger's head
with one blow of
his sharp sword.
The little cub, all the
time laughing unseen
behind the
tree.

The Kobunsha's Japanese Fairy Tale Series.

Published by the KOBUNSHA, 2, Minami Saegicho, TOKYO.

www.ingramcontent.com/pod-product-compliance
Lightning Source LLC
Chambersburg PA
CBHW021551270326
41930CB00008B/1460